Constance Owen Faunt Le Roy Runcie

Poems, Dramatic and Lyric

Constance Owen Faunt Le Roy Runcie

Poems, Dramatic and Lyric

ISBN/EAN: 9783744797573

Printed in Europe, USA, Canada, Australia, Japan

Cover: Foto ©Thomas Meinert / pixelio.de

More available books at **www.hansebooks.com**

POEMS

DRAMATIC AND LYRIC

BY

CONSTANCE FAUNT LE ROY RUNCIE
AUTHOR OF "DIVINELY LED"

NEW YORK AND LONDON
G. P. PUTNAM'S SONS
The Knickerbocker Press
1888

DEDICATED

TO

MY HUSBAND

REV. JAMES RUNCIE, D.D.

———

To you I inscribe this little book. To you whose
faithful love, noble example, and Christian virtues have
made it a delight to be your wife. If any one shall
reap pleasure in the perusal of these simple little poems,
it shall be because to you I owe these happy years, which
made it, under God, possible for me to have leisure in
our married life, while in the midst of your own most
busy and useful work.

CONSTANCE FAUNT LE ROY RUNCIE.

CHRIST CHURCH RECTORY,
ST. JOSEPH, MISSOURI.

CONTENTS.

	PAGE
TWO GIFTS—POETRY AND SONG	I
ANSELMO, THE PRIEST	3
DEMETRIUS	II
CHRIST AND THE SOUL	2I
DECEIVED	23
THE WOMAN HE LOVES	25
SILENCE AND THE SEA	28
THY LOVER	29
PRAYER	3I
I HAVE LET IT GO	33
THE SPANISH MOTHER	35
OH, TO BE AT REST!	43
MEMORY'S PICTURE	45
FORGIVENESS	47
FIRST LOVE	48
THE INTERPRETER OF SONG	50
IF I MAY	52
THIS WOULD I DO	54
PROUD ANGUISH	56
CLAUDIA	59
WHOSE SIN?	65

	PAGE
GREETING	73
I HOLD MY HEART SO STILL	75
A SIMPLE BALLAD	76
YOU AND I	80
DOVE OF PEACE	82
THE FLOWER COQUETTE	83
IN THE WOODS	84
I ONLY WAIT	86
FLOWERS	89
ALAS!	91
YOU WOKE ME	92
KNOWN UNTO GOD	93
BROKEN FRIENDSHIP	98

TWO GIFTS.

POETRY AND SONG.

————

A star came falling from the sky,
  I caught the lovely thing ;
It was a song sent from on high,
  Flashed from an angel's wing.
From one of heaven's golden harps
  This little song came straying ;
It stole into my very heart,
  As if I had been praying.
Who sang it first, I do not know,
  Nor how it lost its way ;
I only caught it to my heart,
  And whispered to it, "Stay."

A dainty floweret at my feet,
  From out the ground came peeping,

Within the snow-white chaliced cup,
    A Poem lay there sleeping.
'T was sent to me from Mother Earth,
    By these most lovely hands ;
I caught it to my heart of hearts,
    And heard its sweet demands.
Who wrote it first, I do not know,
    Nor how it lost its way ;
I found it in the flower's heart,
    And whispered to it, "Stay."

No longer mine alone are these,
    This flower and this song,
I give them as they came to me,
    To you they may belong.
I only listened with my soul,
    I only loved them well,
And plucked the flower as it grew,
    And saw the star that fell.
Who sang—who wrote—I do not know,
    Nor how they lost their way ;
I only caught them to my heart,
    And whispered to them, "Stay."

ANSELMO, THE PRIEST.

SCENE—*A Roman Catholic cathedral, dimly lighted.*

DRESS—*The priest's robes.*

ANSELMO, THE PRIEST.

With the shades of evening gathering around him—
alone—in his dimly lighted and deserted church, Anselmo lies prostrate at the foot of the cross, writhing in
spiritual agony. He speaks :

"Shall I, a priest of God, live on in sin?
　O heart of mine, break, break, but own it not ;
Thy vows remember ; consecrated soul,
　Accept the stripes laid on thee quivering hot.

"It is too much ; too much is asked of me,
　I have no strength ; forgive, O mighty God !
For I am spent with oft repeated fasts,
　And faint beneath the chastening of thy rod.

" I saw her here again, I always see her
　The lovely face that ever haunts me so ;

5

'T was early Mass—were others here beside her?
Alas! I saw but her; I do not know.

"Lo! at the sacred cross I 'll kneel and pray;
It may be Christ, the Son of God, will hear,
And drive the Devil from my hungry heart,
And let me feel His Holy Presence near.

"They tell me I can sing; men praise my voice;
They say 't is rare, that people come to hear;
And once, when chanting through the aisle, we came
Close where she sat, I saw her shed a tear.

"So close were we my vestments touched her sleeve;
I thrilled with hottest joy, and walked on panting.
Her lover! yes! although she only thought
It was the priest absorbed in holy chanting.

"O mercy, Lord!—have mercy on my soul!
I am the priest; shall I forget my vow?
I will do penance—fast—keep vigil—pray—
If only I may claim thy help now, now.

" For Satan comes ; I hear his whisper vile :
  Why this I 've often thought before—yes, yes—
That I might use this voice men call so grand,
  And win, with her, both honor and success.

" Then I will go—I 'll fly this very night !
  O eyes so dear ! O lips ! O form divine !
O ecstasy of bliss ! surpassing sweet
  The hope to win ! ye must—ye shall be mine !

*   *   *   *   *   *

" I must have fainted here, and lain all night
  Prone at the sacred feet on floor of stone,
For I am giddy still—the early dawn
  Doth barely show me church, silent and lone.

" This is a holy day ; the faithful soon
  Will come sins to confess ; I must within
And hear the weary wrongs of souls, and then
  Absolve them from their heavy yoke of sin.

" For I am still the priest ! Last night I dreamed ;
  Tho' faint and spent, tho' pitifully weak,

No food shall pass my lips this day, no words
Aught save my sacred office bids me speak.

" This kind goeth not forth except men fast
And pray ; then hear me while I fast and pray,
Absolving me from sin.   I will not leave
These sacred walls upon this holy day.

" But some one comes, some poor, sin-stricken soul,
Who through the early dawn doth softly steal,
And seeks in holy church confessional,
On penitential stool to meekly kneel.

" My daughter, what is this you would confess—
A sinful love ?—(O heart, be still !) And he
A priest you say ?—I stifle !—help me breathe !
A priest ? Oh no, no, no,—this shall not be !

" This is a mortal sin, pray God,—I can
No more—a sudden sickness hath come o'er,—
Go ! daughter, go ! yet stay ! 't is mortal sin,
Yet tell me which, *which* priest, I do implore !

" Hush, whisper low his name, Father Anselmo,
  The pale and holy priest of God, whose voice
Is more than seraph-sweet, whose glorious song
  Must make the angels, high in heaven, rejoice.

" 'T is she ! my love !—'t is she ! Anselmo I——
  She loves me, her sweet lips have breathed it low ;
I think my heart-strings break, I drink her breath,
  I cannot speak,—she must, in silence, go.

" I hear her weeping—mercy !—mercy, Christ !
  How can I let her go ?   One word, O Lord,
To tell my love, I love ;—one little word,—
  Then take my heart and plunge thy flaming sword !

" She 's weeping still !—Ha !—mercy, mercy !
  O my love !—O merciful Heaven, hear !
Help, help, help ! my heart is dying, O Christ !
  How can I live and not kiss 'way that tear ?

" Weep on, weep on, my heart is crucified,
  And nailed upon the cross, stabbed through and
    through !

I cannot move, I am a priest of God,
   And to my sacred vows I will be true."

     *   *   *   *   *   *

'T was yet scarce day when in the church came chanting
   The Orders holy—no other soul was there ;
They, later, found their young and gifted brother
   Anselmo, dead in his confessional chair.

DEMETRIUS.

II

DRAMATIS PERSONÆ.

PHILIP—*The Second King of Macedonia.*

DEMETRIUS—*The Crown-Prince.*

PERSES—*Disinherited son of the king.*

PRINCESS ZÖE—*Betrothed to Demetrius.*

The GAOLER.

TIME—*In the reign of Philip II. of Macedonia.*

SCENE—*A prison with a couch of straw.*

COSTUME—*Greek dress worn by royalty.*

DEMETRIUS.

DEMETRIUS—*in Prison.*

I do not understand.   Why am I here?
  A prince of Macedonia in prison thrust?
Imperial Rome! hath she a hand in this?
  No—no—I will my king and father trust.

He loves me!   Why, 't was but this very day
  I felt his large heart beat, and saw a tear
Race down his cheek, as in his arms I lay
  Wrapped in a close embrace; I will not fear,

But sleep in peace.   Yet, first I thank thee, gods,
  That once again I breathe my native air,
Once more have felt my mother's gentle kiss,
  And met, once more, my love with golden hair.

13

It was a royal greeting they gave me,—
  My kingly sire upon his throne of state—
While crowding round, in sumptuous attire,
  Were Macedonia's nobles, and her great.

Then swore I knightly troth on bended knee,
  And took the oath of fealty to the crown ;
And here again I swear I will be true,
  And live for country, honor, and renown !

This is my dungeon ; let me for the night
  Feel what it is in prison low to lie ;
Should I become a king, I then may know,
  And spare unhappy souls brought here to die.

Yes, I will rest me here ; this couch of straw
  Shall be to me a paradise of dreams :
My Zöe, I will fondly think of thee,
  How in thine eyes the holy love-light gleams.

Ha !—hark, that grating noise—See ! in the lock
  The rusty key slow turns. It must be he,

My father and my king—he loves me true,
And comes at last to set Demetrius free.

[*Enter* PERSES.]

Thou ! Perses ! Thou ! my brother, is it thou ?
Where is the king ? Why send me from the ranks ?
Our royal father waits ?—Come, let us go—
Thou bringest my release ? Thanks, Perses, thanks.

Why, what is this ? You wear no friendly smile.
Am I, the prince, a prisoner of the state ?
What means this, brother ? Speak ! and let me know
What have I done deserving of this fate ?

You tender me the cup ? Ha ! this means death !
The king decrees I shall drink this to-night ?
My brother ! are you mad ? I—the prince,
And Macedonia's heir ?—Hear I aright ?

The king, my father, orders me to die ?
'T is 'gainst all nature ! Perses, with me bear,

For I am dazed—my poor brain reels—I know
Not what I say—I—I stifle—give me air!

'T is passed! Hand me the cup! This weakness ill
Becomes the prince Rome taught self to deny.
The king decrees? Enough! His wish is law,
Go take this word : Demetrius will die.

[*Exit* PERSES.]

He 's gone!—I am alone and facing death :
I will compose myself, kneel here and pray.
Farewell to all this world holds dear to me ;
O king, farewell, thy son shall well obey.

Now, who comes here in this my last sad hour?
Once more the bolt withdraws! Oh, it must be,
The king sends a reprieve!—I live!—I live!
I thank thee, God—'t is rapture to be free!

[*Enter* PRINCESS ZÖE.]

Almighty powers! Zöe—thou, love—thou?
Or is my brain all crazed, and I behold

An angel in my prison ?   Not till now
  Did I know all the anguish hearts can hold.

O love, love, love, why camest my Zöe here ?
  Thou knowest I must die ; and now the pain
How keen !   To see thee—hold thee—lose thee—Zöe,
  My heart must burst with this last cruel strain !

How can I die—ye gods—how can I die ?
  Go, Zöe, go ! my love, for dost thou stay,
My heart pants with full life, and I forget
  Rome taught the son his father to obey.

What 's this my Zöe whispers soft and low ?
  " Demetrius, fly ! O fly with me, my own !
For I must die if thou art brought to death ;
  I cannot live and meet the world alone.

" The gaoler has been won by me with gold,
  Haste ! haste ! in agony of soul, I pray,
And, on my knees, beseech thee fly with me ;
  Demetrius, my love, haste, haste away."

Now may the gods on high give me the strength
Enchantment to resist.   This is mine hour
Of mortal anguish.   Zöe, my own, my sweet,
Try not Demetrius beyond his power.

Wouldst thou have me betray my princely word?
I promised to the king that I would die :
But then ! just Heaven ! those tears burn up my soul.
'T is more than I can bear—I yield—I fly—

The road, thou say'st, is free ?   Come, Zöe, come !
How sweet thou art, how beautiful thine eyes !
O never breathed a truer soul than thine,
And thou art mine !   O glory fit for skies !

But halt !   My heart cease thy full beat of life,
And stab with pain no more, for I must die ;
One kiss, my own,—go ! hide those tears from me,
Lest I should yield again, and with thee fly.

[She snatches the cup and drinks.]

O Gods ! stay, Zöe, stay ! what hast thou done !
Drank of that cup ?   'T is poison swift, 't is death—

Help! help! she dies! O gaoler, she is gone!
Didst hear? She blessed me with her dying breath.

[*She dies.*]

Give me the cup—where pressed she her sweet lips?
Show me the spot, and on my knees I 'll drink—
My Zöe—angel!—thou hast died for me,
And where thou goest thy lover will not shrink.

So—I have drained the very last dark drop,
And fiery serpents in my veins leap high :

[*Enter the king.*]

Is this the king? Too late—yet this is joy!
My father, on thy heart, now let me die.

[*Dies.*]

CHRIST AND THE SOUL.

Not in mine own, but in thy strength, O Lord,
    Have I found peace.
The fight was hard, and only thou dost know
    How hard—thou !
Then had I fainted, vanquished by my pain,
    When came release,
And once more, Lord, I freely breathe again,
    And bare my brow
Unto my life, and walk with upright step.
    Thou art my friend :
I give thee smile for smile, and love for love.
    I will defend
Thy holy cause, here on our earth 'mong men :
    For me—defend
My weak and sinful cause high up in heaven,.
    Before my God,

And say : " She fainted ; but the fight was hard,
    And she sore pressed."
Then walk beside me nearer still, O Christ,
    And I am blest.

DECEIVED.

It died hard, this love of mine for thee ;
    'T was long in dying.
It took strong hands to break, at last, the stem
    Upon which grew
The flower of my large and patient love.
    Men said of me :
" This woman builds a castle of enchantment,
    In which she keeps
Her friends, where they may walk in bright attire,
    All robed in virtues
They do not own,—but her imagination
    Hangs about them."
They said this thing of thee : " You think him good,
    Wholly unselfish ;
You think him gentle, merciful, and kind,
    A very prince,

And full of noble gratitude, and far above
A common man."
Then smiled we both—they only in derision,
I—in content
And firm conviction that I knew the man.
I knew you not.
It was not you I loved, for you *are* selfish,
Hard, and cold,
Implacable, ungentle, and vindictive.
I love you not,
And yet—so strong, so firm was my affection,
That, as I said,
My love died hard—it took strong hands to kill.
It now lies dead.
And you are still yourself—'t is only I
Who lose the friend,
For whom I built so fair and rich a castle.
The man lived not,
Except in mine own mind, begot of God.

THE WOMAN HE LOVES.

Do you know why he loves this woman
  Apart from all the rest?
Because of the strong, deep beauty
  Her nature is possessed.

Because of the shining soul
  That smiles from out her eyes,
And the power of Truth's bright glory
  That on her forehead lies.

Because deep in her heart
  So gentle a softness lives,
That whomsoever offends,
  She still loves and forgives.

Because light as a feather
  She takes the ills of life,

And when the stab *must* come,
She hides away the knife.

Dipping her brush in sunshine,
The colors only choosing
That paint life fair and bright;
The rest her soul refusing.

Because of her bold free thought;
Unfettered by what man thinks,
She takes the chain of prejudice
And breaks apart the links.

Because of her childlike faith,
Which makes her strong and sure.
Of Heaven—believing much,
Then much she can endure.

Because at the purest fountain
Of love she drinks so deep,
That she gives and takes unstinted
The treasures others keep.

Because of the moral grandeur
  Of her soul, that dares to be
Itself, above man's law,
  Godlike, brave, and free.

Because her words and actions
  Are all her very own,
Not taking from those around her
  Their coloring and their tone.

You know now why he loves her,
  Exalted above the rest,
Why, holding fast her friendship,
  He counts himself so blest.

SILENCE AND THE SEA.

SONG.[1]

The great sea rolls between us,
And silence wide and deep,
But my soul unto thine
Its faithful troth doth keep.
My love is like a flower
That form and color hideth,
And only by its fragrance
You mark where it abideth.
The night wind sighs around me,
And blends its undertone
With this my song I sing—
I sing to thee alone.
It tells thee I remember,
It whispers thoughts of thee,
Altho' there roll between us
Deep silence and the sea.

[1] Set to music by the author.

THY LOVER.

More lovely to me art thou
  Than rose on thy breast,
More precious to him who loves,
  Than gold of the West.

I vow I cannot discern
  'Twixt heaven and thee,
Since lo! gazing upward, thine eyes
  Are all that I see.

I cannot tell if it be music
  Or only thy laugh,
Whether thou smilest—or sun shines
  On my behalf.

Bloweth the south wind low,
  Or is it thy touch?

These tokens all tell thee, my sweet,
I love thee so much.

Did I pray, or was it thy whisper
Shaking my soul ?
Bringing me nearer to Heaven,
And under control ?

Did I dream, or was it an angel
Leaving the skies ?
Who borrowed thy lips and thy hair,
Who borrowed thine eyes ?

O I love thee, I love thee ! I love
By night and by day,
And had I a thousand more tongues
'T is all I should say.

PRAYER.

O lift me out of self, and out of passion,
 Let me forget to be at war with good,
And like to them above, of purer fashion,
 The great—serene—angelic brotherhood.

Am I cut to the soul—misunderstood—
 Or fretted with the little things of life,
Which daily rise a countless multitude,
 And daily cause me never ending strife ?

And shall I grieve when wishes vainly perish,
 Or battle with this deeply wounded pride,
With all the wrong it would in secret cherish,
 With all the bitterness it seeks to hide ?

A thousand times O no ! These are not mine,
 But thine, O Christ ! Their burden killed,

And I live only when I give them thee,
   And with thy gracious peace, instead, are filled.

A peace that was not mine by right of birth,
   O soul ! exchange quick with thy Lord ! for heaven
He gives thee, haste ! give thine ills of earth,
   And lightly rise with this thy new soul-leaven.

I HAVE LET IT GO.

The dearest hope I had,
> At last, I 've let it go,
> I would not hold it longer.
My trembling hands tho' loth,
> Unloosed their loving clasp,
> And fate becomes the stronger.

I loved my idol so
> As woman-love
> Knows how to worship ever.
It was not meant that I
> Should keep and hold this love,
> And so, at last, I sever
Ties that bind me like
> The sinews of my heart,
> My very flesh and blood,

33

Part of myself, almost
    My very life, I yield
    Because I know I should.

And so—I 've let it go ;
    And now what shall I do
    To keep my heart from breaking ?
Will knowing that I 've acted
    As my conscience speaks
    Prevent my soul from aching ?

But no ! I will not ask ;
    Be quiet, trembling hands,
    That seek to clasp again
The treasure so well loved.
    It may be Peace, at last,
    Shall take the place of Pain.

THE SPANISH MOTHER.

TIME—*During the Inquisition in Spain.*

SCENE—*In a dungeon.*

COSTUME—*Spanish dress of a lady of high degree.*

THE SPANISH MOTHER.

At last, at last, O Christ, they bring me here.
   Give me the strength to triumph o'er my fears ;
A woman weak who staggers—one, whose grief
   Has burned up in her heart and eyes all tears.

I had a happy home where there was peace,
   And you—O my love—they 've taken you !
In heaven only shall I meet again
   The husband God gave me, so brave and true.

I will not shrink—see ! see ! the marks are here
   Of their hot tongs which seared my poor wrists.
Their dreadful torture lingers in my brain,
   Of how the heated iron burns and twists.

No—no—I will not faint, but kneel down here
   And think of God ; perhaps, in spite of youth,

I may be firm—help purify his Church,
  And die, if needs I must, for God and truth.

Can I forget that night, when, as we sat
  Close side by side, my husband's tender smile
Sank in my heart, and low he spoke the words :
  "Be strong, my own—'t is only for a while."

And then they tore him from my clinging arms,
  To thrust him in a dungeon—tortured him—
O God—O God—I think I hear him cry,
  As on that dreadful wheel they broke each limb !

I shall go mad ! no, no, I must not think,
  But pray.   Give, give me strength, Almighty God,
That I may feel thine everlasting arms,
  That I may humbly kiss thy chastening rod !

And then my child !   Ha !—I—I—
  I cannot breathe ! O that once more the bliss
Were given me to see again my boy,
  And press upon his little lips one kiss.

They come ! my Judges.   Lo ! they come !
  I hear the grating key.   Now help me, Lord !
Give me the power that I resist their bribes,
  Let me defend thy pure and holy word.

[*Enter Child.*]

My child !—my sweetest, sweetest darling child,
  Here, here, quick on my heart, my precious boy !
O happy mother that I may again
  Kiss thee ! I thank them, thank them for this joy !

God bless them, bless their kind and friendly hearts
  That they give me my child back to my arms.
I will pray for their souls ; my prison now
  Doth lose its ghastly, terrible alarms.

What says my little Carlos ?   Speak, my boy :
  " O mother, must I die when you can save ?
For if you will but speak and tell the priests
  You love their holy church—I will be brave

" And they will set us free, for they now send
  Me here to tell you this.   O mother, fly !

'T is only to believe as they believe—
　And then we both go free ! O must we die ?"

O God ! mercy !—Christ have mercy—mercy—
　They make me slay my child. Hear me pray.
I am not strong enough for this—my lamb—
　Kiss me and live. My child I cannot slay.

　　　　[Enter Priests—The Inquisitors.]

They come, they come, see, here I fall and kneel
　Before you, priests of God. O spare my child !
Take me—have mercy on my little one—
　Take me before my sorrow drives me wild.

And lead me to the stake ! Here are my hands—
　Quick ! quick ! but spare my child, O spare him
　　priests !
Slay, slay me ! burn me ! tear me limb from limb,
　But let my child go free. What ! are ye beasts

That would kill children innocent and pure,
　And mangle their soft flesh ? O listen not

To my wild words, but spare my only son,
 And throw me to the flames now scorching hot!

And you shall see I will not make a cry,
 But go with you ; my spirit shall not flinch.
Ye priests of God, O let my child go free,
 Take me and let the fire burn inch by inch!

They drag my child away ! he calls his mother !
 Oh ! oh ! oh ! kind priests—one kiss,
The last, last kiss before my child is gone !
 The door is shut—open !—open !—this—

This is more than I can bear ! my baby !—O
 Almighty God ! they 'll slay my child !
And I—I might have saved us both, one word !
 But then !—avaunt, Satan ! by thee beguiled,

I would lose my own soul, and meet no more
 My sainted ones in heaven. O Lord, defend !
O God, sustain and give me strength that I
 May hold the truth until the last sad end.

What 's this ? can I be dying ?   Ah !—my heart—
  Be with thy servant, Lord : this must be death :
I thank thee—husband ! soon, my love, we meet !
  My God, I praise thee with my dying breath.

[*Dies.*]

OH, TO BE AT REST.

———

SONG.[1]

Oh, to be at peace,
  Oh, to be at rest,
Oh, to sleep at last,
  The long sleep of the blest !

Oh, to cease to weep,
  Oh, to cease the strife,
Oh, to leave the weariness
  Of what we know of life !

Oh, to leave the tear,
  Oh, to leave the sigh,
Oh, to wish no more
  Only the wish to die !

[1] Set to music by the author.

43

The aching heart at peace,
The weary brain at rest,
The tired hands but folded
Over the empty breast.

Away !—only away !
Beholding God's dear face,
With nothing but great peace,
And everlasting grace.

MEMORY'S PICTURE.

My love came through the door, and lo!
   Her very form and face,
So purely simple, seemed to glow
   With new, peculiar grace.

Her dress was black, and made of gauze,
   Which veiled but did not hide
Her perfect arms, so softly white,
   They with the lily vied.

The crimson flowers at her throat
   Were all the jewels worn,
Except her eyes, which shone above
   With light that was love-born.

She held within her graceful hands
   Her hat, which, hanging down,

Broke with its strings of ribbon bright
The dead black of her gown.

She was a picture standing there,
Altho' she did not know it,
My love, with earnest, truthful brow,
My dreamer and my poet.

I would have fallen at her feet,
I could have worshipped there,
So graceful in her flowing robes,
But that I did not dare.

I in my very soul and heart,
Would paint her if I could,
As coming through the door that night
We saw her as she stood.

FORGIVENESS.

Because it is divine
    To know how to forgive,
    I 'll be divine,
And wipe from out my troubled heart
The memory of this sin of thine.

Ah, yes ! I will forgive—
    But not of thy deserving ;
    Thou deservest nought,
Except that I should hate this wrong
To me and mine, that thou hast wrought.

I will forgive as I
    Hope one day to be forgiven,
    And put away
This human ache to hate thee most
Intensely.   I will forgive and pray.

FIRST LOVE.

O holy love ! O beautiful and sacred
Love. The evening shadows stealing out
To sea, or night-bloom of the skies, fall not
More softly, than the breath of a first and holy
Love upon the young and trembling heart.
Unconscious first—

        Then as a dream, and then—
The great awakening ! O moments fleeting ! O hour
That cannot stay ! O youth ! O love ! O soul !
Never again to be the same ! Hast thou
Laid this thy gift, thy gift unspeakable,
Here at my feet ? For this, O friend, I thank thee.
Thou crown'st me queen, indeed ; I am more fair
Because I wear the jewel of thy first love.
I will arise and purify myself,
Will kneel and say unto my God : " My Father,

Hold, hold me closer to thy heart, for I
Would learn of thee, how I may meet and keep
This noble treasure of a first, great love."
And then into the quiet keeping of a
Mighty trust, I will exalt, and place
This priceless gift forever and forever.

THE INTERPRETER OF SONG.

He stands composed before them all,
  With grave, and serious air,
A deep light burning in his eyes,
  The young face calm and fair.
His hands are clasped as if in prayer,
  His chest is broadly thrown,
The head is raised with dignity,
  As if it wore a crown !
Then part the lips in richest song,
  And majesty of tone ;
He sings as if the melody
  Were all his very own.
His soul is seeking for the truth,
  His voice with passion rings ;
He thinks not of himself, but stands
  Creating as he sings.

50

O glory of a life that can
　So nobly hearts allure,
And win them, through the charm of song,
　To love the grand and pure.

IF I MAY.

I will not take the joy which brings a sorrow,
  If I may,
  Put both away.
I will not learn to love a smile, a voice,
  If glance and tone,
  Once mine alone,
Shall in some hour lose all their strongest power.

I will not choose that in my life may come
  The deep unrest,
  Tho' it were blest
With joy ; for I would wish my soul should be
  As if asleep,
  If God will keep
Me safe within his holy arms, and let
  Me never know

The bitter woe
Of what it means to say—" *I must forget.*'

PART SECOND.

Yes ! I will welcome all, nor will refuse,
       Or joy, or pain,
       If I may gain,
Through all the changing light and deepening shade,
       One step nearer,
       One hope dearer,
That out of all my soul may rise the purer,
       And find the path,
       Which ever hath
Brought them, who suffer, on their way the surer.

Yes—give me all that I may be the richer,
       And may know
       Both joy and woe
Shall only weave for me that brighter dress,
       Which I shall wear,
       When I may bear,
Of God's own image, the divine impress.

THIS WOULD I DO.

If I were a rose,

This would I do :

I would lie upon the white neck of her I love,

And let my life go out upon the fragrance

Of her breath.

If I were a star,

This would I do :

I would look deep down into her eyes,

Into the eyes I love, and learn there

How to shine.

If I were a truth strong as the Eternal One,

This would I do :

I would live in her heart, in the heart

I know so well, and

Be at home.

If I were a sin,

  This would I do :

I would fly far away, and tho' her soft hand

In pity were stretched out, I would not stay, but fly,

    And leave her pure !

PROUD ANGUISH.

Take away your hand
               From my life,
Turn aside ! and so—
               Come no more !
You may go, and leave me
               To hide
The heart you have bruised
               To the core.
Take from me the sweet
               Cruel eyes,
Take also the touch
               That can thrill.
Go !—leave me my life,
               Only leave me,
Before the whole woman
               You kill.

56

You dared to look into

        Too closely

The innermost shrine

        Of my soul ;

You entered the

        " Holy of Holies "

Not wearing the

        High-priestly stole.

You felt not some places

        Are sacred,

Your shoes you still kept

        On your feet,

While Moses came walking

        Unsandaled,

The burning-unburned

        Bush to meet.

But you ! you trod

        On my heart ;

Your hands were rough

        And were bold,

You gave me the dross

Of your nature,
While I gave you nothing
But gold.
Pass on ! only leave me
To silence,
That I may recover
My breath,
Awhile ——— ere I go to
My grave,
Forgiving you only
In death.

CLAUDIA.

An Historic Incident in the Life of the last of the Claudii.

On sterile shore of some lone sea,
　Whose walls of granite rock,
For ages fretted carelessly,
　The wild waves seemed to mock.
Where cold and bleak the night wind blew,
　And sea-gull hoarsely screamed,
And deeper still the shadows grew,
　And whiter the wave-crest gleamed.
'T was there they laid the infant down
　Upon its cold, hard bed,
Banished by her own father's frown,
　Who wished the child were dead.
Rome's emperor he—a Claudii,
　Detested as a race,

59

Now doomed his infant child to die,
   Its mother to disgrace.
Urgalania she—who once as queen
   Had sat on Cæsar's throne,
Now driven forth with frantic spleen,
   To wander all alone.
They tore the babe from out her arms,
   They drove her from the city,
And Rome, once proud of all her charms,
   Now had for her no pity.
Polybius bore the sleeping child
   Unto the lonely sea,
Its innocence almost beguiled
   So hard a man as he.
But Pallas, colder than the rocks,
   Marched swiftly by his side,
The pity shown he sternly mocks
   Polybius fain would hide.
And as they neared the fatal shore,
   All desolate and wild,
Amid the ocean's ceaseless roar,
   They stripped the lovely child.

And, naked, left it there to die
  Upon the cold hard stone,
Beneath a wild tempestuous sky,
  Unheeded and alone.
They turned them from the cruel spot,
  They strode in haste away ;
Imperial Rome they once more sought ;
  The babe unnoticed lay.
A princess born—of lofty line,
  The infant Claudia—she
Whose royal birth had been the sign
  Of joy and revelry.
The heavy night came closely down,
  The crested waves leapt high,
The ocean's roar could scarcely drown
  That feeble wailing cry.
And hours long this piteous moan
  Pierced the midnight air,
But hushed at last the sobbing tone
  When morning dawnèd fair.
As wide and bright o'er land and sea,
  Rushed up the radiant sun,

And, meeting death thus smilingly,
    There lay the little one.
A marble statue full of grace,
    Colder than its bed,
A smile of peace upon its face,
    It scarcely seemèd dead.
The glittering sunbeams lingered there
    To paint it with a blush,
And kissing lips, and brow, and hair,
    Left over all a hush.

But who is this with haggard face,
    With wild and frantic air,
Searching in this lonely place
    For something she 's lost there ?
'T is Urgalania, the mother—she
    Once Rome's imperial queen !
And wife of Claudius—he
    Of dark and hideous mien.
She saw the babe upon the ground,
    She dashed upon her knees,

With gasping and half-choking sound
  The child she fain would seize.
She clasped the cold form to her breast,
  She chafed both hands and feet,
With eager lips she fondly pressed
  The limbs, to her, so sweet.
But all in vain—all, all in vain,
  The little life had fled,
And piercing to her maddened brain
  The thought came, it was dead.
She fell upon her knees once more,
  She raised her hands on high,
She cursed all Rome, from shore to shore,
  She cursed the Claudii.
Then, springing up with sudden start,
  As if again to flee,
She laid the child close on her heart,
  And leaped into the sea!

WHOSE SIN?

SCENE—*The bedroom of a young girl. A coffin covered with flowers.*

COSTUMES—*That of an old man, gray hair and beard.*

WHOSE SIN?

Here leave me with my dead, I thank you all,
  You have been kind since my deep trouble came ;
But yet of her now lying cold in death,
  To you her memory will be linked with shame.

So I would be alone. . . . You have done well,
  And made my child look fair, with leaf and flower.
Perhaps you shed some tears, yet in your minds
  A scornful thought against my child will lower.

Yet, once again, I thank you—leave me now.
  Thank God ! they 've gone.   Am I in truth alone ?
I may kneel, now, and ask that for her sin,
  The loving Saviour's blood will sure atone.

Yes ! I will kneel and lay my gray head down
  Beside the fairest face that ever smiled ;

So like her mother—she had the same blue eyes,
  The same soft hair, and brow so calm and mild.

Oh ! well I do recall her wedding night,
  How sweet, how like a fairy—no thought of fear,
She came down from this room in this same dress
  She now wears lying in her coffin drear.

She blushed and smiled and hung around my neck ;
  "Oh ! how you 'll miss me, father," whispered she,
" For all our lives together we have been,
  And oh ! you 've been so good, so kind to me."

And then they told her it was time to go ;
  It seemed as tho' I must forever kiss her.
"Be good to this dear child," I said to him,
  "For oh ! my poor old heart will sorely miss her."

Her husband—damn him! curse him!—broke her heart—
  He broke my child's poor heart—he struck her hands
Which she held up before him, weeping sore ;
  He had no pity, but mocked at her demands.

'T was then she asked the man of God to pray,
  For she had summoned us to hear her tale,
Her husband, father, priest, on her poor knees
  She crouched before us trembling, wan and pale.

" Father," she cried, " my father, plead for me,
  Husband, look not so stern, but hear me speak ;
I know that I have sinned, I 've wronged you all,
  I ask for pardon ; husband, I was weak.

" You left me all alone ; I was so young ;
  My heart craved love ; you did not see :
Temptation came, you did not seem to care ;
  And so I fell—ah ! husband, pity me !

" For I repent—O God ! I do repent !
  Say, say you can forgive me ; pray for me, pray !
Ah ! what is this ?   My heart has stopped its beats ;
  Perhaps kind death may take this pain away."

Then—as she held her poor beseeching hands
  Up to her husband, and so ceased to speak,

But hung upon his face to read forgiveness,
　　With panting, bated breath and pallid cheek—

He struck her down !   Ha ! I must have air !—
　　Devil ! beast !   Why I will kill him yet !—
He left her days alone ; did he not see
　　Her heart was growing hard at his neglect ?

She was so young, so used to being loved,
　　Her husband—iron-stern—soon seemed to think
She had no claim on him.　Alas ! neglect
　　Drove her, at last, beyond the fatal brink,

And then she made confession—tender soul,
　　And sinking 'neath his blow, fell on her face.
I caught her to my heart, and let him go ;
　　I loved my lamb the more in her disgrace.

'T was long ere she revived ; but when once more
　　The life-blood blushed upon her lovely cheek,
I held her to my heart, I stroked her hair ;
　　She pressed her lips to mine, but did not speak.

Then slipping from my arms she came up here;
  This was her room before her mother died,
And after she was gone I kept it so,
  Exactly as she left it, happy bride.

It was not very long, I heard a sound—
  A fatal sound—I knew it well.—With speed
I flew up to my darling's room—too late!
  O God, forgive my precious child this deed!

See had put on this dress she lies in now—
  Her bridal robe, with roses in her hair;
She looked as she had looked her wedding night,
  So young, so sweet, so sad, so still, and fair,

With that death-wound straight through her broken
    heart.
  She left me all alone—how can I live?
Ha! all grows dark—can this, can this be death?
O God, forgive my child—forgive, forgive!

*   *   *   *   *   *

They found him kneeling by his daughter's bier,
 His gray hair straggling o'er her poor face ;
Both wore the still cold smile of death ;
 Both went away to seek God's loving grace.

GREETING.

Dear love, we come in memory of your birth,
　Your wife, your children, and these your friends,
To keep the feast with sweet and lively mirth,
　In gratitude to Him who birthdays sends.

We know your deeds of loving kindness well,
　We know you have a heart that strong doth feel
The beauty of that Gospel which you tell
　To us who, in the sanctuary, round you kneel.

We know the little children on the street
　Wave you sweet kisses with their dimpled hands,
And smiles of innocence and love do greet
　You on all sides from these gay childish hands.

We know the sick and lonely long to hear
　The words of sympathy and lowly prayer

You bring to dying bedsides, dispelling fear,
And teaching them the loving Father's care.

We know the Poor who shiver without wood,
Who see their children starving, come to you,
Relying on your power to give them food,
Because you *act* your Gospel, pure and true.

We know the doubting Thomas doth also come,
And feareth not that you hold up the rod,
He knows your modest faith, tho' it be dumb
In argument, clings closely to your God.

And now who knows so well your silent worth
As she, your wife, who here, with grateful pride,
Calls in your friends, rejoicing that your birth
Gave her the honor to be your chosen bride !

I HOLD MY HEART SO STILL.

SONG.[1]

I know that thou art God,
  I hold my heart so still,
And say, between my tears,
  I yield me to thy will.
My sins, I know, are many,
  I feel how weak I am,
O Saviour! give to me,
  O give thy blessed calm!
I do not wish to murmur,
  I hold me fast and still,
I only ask to hide my tears,
  And know, O God, thy will.

[1] Set to music by the author.

A SIMPLE BALLAD.

Before her father's cottage door,
    The children often played,
Her eyes were blue, but his were black,
    And he loved the little maid.

She grew in all her beauty wild,
    And sweetly could she sing :
The people said, the world some day
    Would with her praises ring.

They bade her kiss the neighbor-boy
    And say a long farewell ;
They carried her o'er hills away,
    But still he loved her well.

The summers came, the summers went,
    The winters brought their snow,

When forth to find the little maid,
The neighbor-boy would go.

His knapsack on his shoulder,
His love deep in his heart,
His black eyes glistening with the joy
He felt, at last, to start.

He came into a city great,
He heard her sing again,
She wore a dress of satin white,
And roses looped her train.

He stood without, the crowd was great,
To see the Prima Donna,
Beside her came a plumèd knight,
Who bore the cross of honor.

She smilèd with her eyes of blue
Into his eyes of black,
But knew him not and passed him by,
A peasant with knapsack !

The night was dark, the night was wild,
    The stars shone cold and clear,
He wandered with his broken heart
    Off to mountains drear.

He sat him down he cared not where,
    So cold was he and weary ;
He fell asleep and dreamed a dream,
    So bright it was and cheery.

The little maid and he together
    In church knelt side by side ;
He was the happy bridegroom gay,
    And she the joyous bride.

She wore a dress of satin white,
    And roses looped her train ;
The organ rolled and upward bore
    Its glorious refrain.

And then he woke—the mountains drear
    Rose up against the sky,

The night-wind pierced him to the soul,
  And bore away his cry :

" O let me dream this dream again,
  This heavenly dream once more."
And, smiling with his icy lips,
  He dreamed just as before.

The snow came whirling down and down,
  The everlasting hills
Stood round about the neighbor-boy,
  While icy darkness fills

The air and sky. But never more
  The neighbor-boy would wake ;
He sleepeth well, and still the heart
  That broke for her dear sake.

YOU AND I.

Friend ! when you felt the baleful ecstasy of power
    To make me feel,
Why took you then my heart, to use it as a stone
    To sharpen steel ?
You saw I was much moved at all you felt and said,
    And ever since
It is with no fine sparing hand you wield the knife,
    And see me wince
Beneath the glittering blade.   Is this noble in you ?
    Is this a friend ?
To be so stern, so hard ; to take a fault that 's mine,
    And not defend,
But strip my woman's pride, which is a bridal veil,
    Unpitying take
My sin and bear it quivering 'neath your ruthless eyes,
    And coldly make

Me say " 'T is mine."   To you I would not, if I could,
　　Ungentle be.
Your fault I 'd take, and fathoms deep would hide it
　　From the world and me !

DOVE OF PEACE.

SONG.[1]

I would that the dove of Peace
   Might find her home in my breast,
And, folding her gentle wings,
   Might make of my heart her nest.
I would that I might not hear
   The complaining voice of my soul,
Nor the thunder of the deep waters,
   As wave upon wave doth roll.
I would that my feet might walk
   On the road that leadeth higher,
Instead of standing and sinking
   Low down in the cruel mire.
O God of my life! come to me,
   And bless thy weary child!
In the palm of thine hand, O hide me,
   Quiet and reconciled!

[1] Set to music by the author.

THE FLOWER-COQUETTE.

Do'st see this dainty flower ?
  Within her fragrant cup
She lured a ray of sun-gold,
  And fairly used him up.
She held him fast a prisoner,
  Made of herself a prism,
Dividing all his colors,
  Anointed with holy chrism
Each charming velvet petal.
  Was not she cunning, though,
To steal his colors and paint herself
  A dainty flower rainbow ?

IN THE WOODS.

Come not with me, but let me go alone,
    Into the woods to-day ;
Not one of you I want, but undertone
    Of what the hills may say.
No voice I wish to hear, except the bird,
    Or breathings of the grass,
Or whispering leaves by wind so gently stirred,
    As 'neath I pass.

The pulsing of the sinless hearts around,
    Of insect, tree, or flower,
Or microscopic moss upon the ground,
    Which lives its little hour,
Is all the sympathy I wish to-day ;
    For friends, the grand old trees

Shall help me lift my silent soul to pray
    With Nature on her knees.

No touch I want, except upon the palm
    The velvet leaf to feel ;
No kiss besides the air so still and calm,
    While there I 'll kneel.
No eyes to look in mine, except the light
    Of heaven's own tender blue,
That offers me an everlasting flight
    To find the good and true.

No ! I would be alone and would commune
    With Nature's spirit only.
To-day the world and I are not in tune,
    My heart is sad and lonely.
Not one of you I want, my spirit's need
    Must search the distant wood,
And there, away in solitude, shall feed
    Upon its highest good.

I ONLY WAIT.

Wait ! give me time,—I cannot breathe
  When I begin this tale ;
My trembling lips can scarcely wreathe
  The words of bitter wail.

You were the very last to cheer
  As we sailed out to sea ;
Remember you the children near,
  The youngest on my knee ?

'T was I who turned and answered then,
  Unthinking, to the cry
Of mother ! mother !—O my God,
  When may I also die !

But I must on. For one whole week
  We sailed without a frown

86

Upon the sky, nor did we reek
  That ships went sometimes down.

Alas ! how can I tell you this ?
  Did you not read ?   You know
Of that wild night ?—O God ! the hiss
  Of storm above—below !

Again I live it through ! feel yet
  The horror of that hour,
When dumb with fright, in cold and wet,
  We felt the dread storm-power !

Amid the screams of mad despair,
  An angel-voice arose.
It was my child, my little Clare,
  Full of high repose.

"Mother," she said, "can no one here
  Pray God to still the storm ?
You 've always taught us He is near
  To shield us from all harm."

My lamb ! my blessed lamb !   No more !
  No time to say the rest,
There came a greater wave which tore
  The darlings from my breast.

Spare me—spare me—all were lost,
  Deep buried in the sea,
Among the souls thus tempest-tossed, .
  The Father left but me.

I went, with all my children sweet,
  Up to the Golden Gate,
To enter there I was not meet,
  So now—*I only wait.*

FLOWERS.

O flowers, flowers, flowers, flowers !
  Come cover me quick all over !
Bury me in your dainty bloom,
Drown me in your sweet perfume,
  For am I not your lover ?
Delicate leaf, and tender color,
  Beautiful shapes so airy,
Blue and gold, and rose and green,
Of velvet soft, with glossy sheen,
  Fit home for variest fairy !

Your beauty links me, lovely ones,
  To higher heavenly powers ;
Ye are my thoughts, my wishes—ye
My songs, my poems, all I see
  Made visible in flowers.

Then come, O come, ye sweetest things,
    And cover me up in bloom ;
Bury me in your green and gold,
Kiss me quick ye colors bold,
    And drown me in perfume !

ALAS!

'T were better had they death between,
Or better each had never seen
How close their two lives might have been,
Than ended so.

YOU WOKE ME.

SONG.[1]

You woke me to music and poetry,
I, you to religion and love ;
Enough !   Go your way and I mine,
We meet in the heavens above.

You were both noble and true,
You gave me your heart's purest love,
And yet !—go your way and I mine,
We meet in the heavens above.

[1] Set to music by the author.

KNOWN UNTO GOD.[1]

See ! yonder stately lordly spire,
    Searching through the sky ;
Which crowns—as flame reveals the fire,
    Cathedral towering high.
Majestic in its grand outline,
    Symmetrical in form,
Rich in its rare and chaste design,
    Proof 'gainst time or storm.

It sanctifies the air around,
    And sets apart a place,
Like heart of man, where God is found,
    To meet him face to face.
The morn is fair—the Archbishop
    Sits in his cap and stole ;

[1] True incident in the building of the great Strasburg cathedral.

He looks with joy upon the walls,
　Which ravish all his soul.

Here, as he sits, a woman comes,
　Bearing within her arms
A stone of wondrous beauty wrought,
　A stone of many charms.
It is the work of her own hands,
　And in it lies her heart ;
"My lord, accept this for thy church,"
　She says, and would depart.

"Stay, woman! this is rarely fine "
　(He cries in eager haste).
"No other stone in all that church
　So beautiful, so chaste.
But how shall workmen place it there
　Where best one may admire ?
Already finish they their work
　Upon the topmost spire !
" Yet this must surely have its place
　Where men its beauty see,

To hide it from the eyes of all,
  I never can agree."

" Nay, but, my lord," the woman said,
  In voice both soft and low,
" If as you say no place is found
  To use it here below,
Then let the workmen bear it up,
  And place it in the spire ;
If men know nothing of this stone,
  And none be to admire,
I know that God above will see,
  His angels will behold
The work I 've put my heart into
  With all my love untold.
And I shall be well satisfied
  To feel that I have given
The best I had, not seen of men,
  But seen of God in heaven."

According as the woman wished,
  They carried up the stone ;

Its beauty hidden from the world,
  Far up in tower lone.
She heeded not the fame thereof
  Might never go abroad,
But satisfied her work to give
  To angels and to God.
And there !—as flame reveals the fire—
  Burning in the sky,
Unto this day, cathedral spire
  Lifteth her work on high.

BROKEN FRIENDSHIP.

I send no greeting ; I do not even feel
Your name forgotten when in prayer I kneel.
You came into my life and passed away,
A troubled dream which flies before the day.

You asked too much.
           There comes, at last, an end
Of what one ought to suffer for a friend.
It then becomes ignoble—self-abase,—
Not sacrifice—pure—holy—full of grace.

I suffered much where now I cannot feel ;
I do not still pretend a friendly zeal
In what you do—or are—or where you go ;
A calm indifference is all I know.

I am not angry even, nor doth there burn
Resentment in my heart !—No !

                      You must learn
How wholly I forgive and can forget.
The sun, upon two friends,

                   Hath simply set.